JUST GO

This book is dedicated to you. If you're reading this, you've impacted my life in some way. Some more directly than others, but every person I've encountered has shaped my career, personality and life in some way.

Without you coming to my performances, watching videos, listening to podcasts, reading the blog and buying this book, I wouldn't be left with much.
Thank you.

GO FOREWORD!

By Dr. Kip Imperato

I've known Chris pretty much my entire life. We went to high school together. We went to college together. And now even though our professional lives have taken two very separate paths, not more than a week ever goes by that we don't call or text each other to make sure we're both getting the maximum creative and productive potential our lives have to offer. Throughout the years, we've easily spent days of combined late night/ early morning hours sitting next to smoldering campfires or on rooftops after the parties have died down, just pondering the intricacies of the universe or trying to think of cool names for t-shirt companies (sometimes both at the same time!) Those discussions could fill an entire book of its own, but many of the themes discovered on those nights will permeate through this one in a much more refined form.

I've been fortunate enough to share a stage or get behind the lens to capture some truly awesome moments because of Chris. I can without a doubt say my life is better for having known him and I'd like to think he'd say the same about me. Friendships like Chris and mine are rare but that's not what this book is about.

For as much as Chris and I have accomplished in our lives, helping each other along the way, the bottom line is that everything we have, and are ever going to have, is because we made one fundamental decision for ourselves. At one point or another we told ourselves: Just Go.

I didn't make Chris a juggler. He didn't make me a veterinarian. I certainly never thought he'd write a book but then again I never thought I'd ever write the fore-word for a book!

But he did it.

I did it.

YOU can do it.

Those clever folks at Nike have been saying it for years, but I actually think "Just Go" is even more empower-ing. Swoosh!

I included the "Dr." in my title for this piece not to sound pretentious or establish any perception of credi-bility like I'm a professor of literature or anything (hell, I'm not even a "real" doctor anyways!) but rather to illustrate the possibilities that attitude, NOT skill can bring about in your life.

I think I'm a smart person and all, but I can assure you that it wasn't intelligence that made me a doctor. I wouldn't say it's Chris' innate dexterity that has made him a great juggler. It's a pretty common thing for me to hear "I always wanted to be a veterinarian." Do you know what I tell those people? Just go... to vet school! It's ACTUALLY that simple. Sure, intelligence and skill will help you get through the things you challenge yourself with, but you have to be willing to take that first step for the opportunity to even learn those skills. I didn't get into a single veterinary school I applied to, but I just kept applying and eventually landed myself in a small school in the Caribbean. I wasn't after prestige. I had a dream and I wasn't going to waste any time achieving it. You HAVE to start SOMEWHERE.

Unknown to me at the time, Chris was overcoming similar adversity pursuing his entertainment career. Was this some sort of strange coincidence? Did we possess some sort of magical superpower? Well, yes and no. It's a superpower alright but it's not magic. Call it perseverance, call it persistence, call it downright stupidity at times, but if you aren't willing to fail, you simply aren't really trying. If you want the right person to say "yes" you have to be willing to hear a lot of "NOs." It sounds really counterintuitive but if you get really good at managing failure, there is no limit to what you can achieve.

I'm glad Chris has taken the time to write this book and share all his ideas with the world. I don't think I realized how lucky I was to have my own personal life coach reminding me of my own superpowers throughout the years until he started writing all this stuff down.

Too many people have had too many great ideas that no one has ever gotten to hear because everyone is too worried about how everyone else will receive their ideas.

I don't think any of Chris' ideas are complete earth-shattering epiphanies but that's the point. You could probably get the same message by listening to Baz Luhrmann's "Everybody's Free (To Wear Sunscreen)" but I guess it comes down to a matter of trust because after all:

"Be careful whose advice you buy, but be patient with those who supply it. Advice is a form of nostalgia, dispensing it is a way of fishing the past from the disposal, wiping it off, painting over the ugly parts and recycling it for more than it's worth."

I trust Chris because he's my friend and I've known him since we were both just weird kids that liked to have a good time. But you can trust him too because if there's one thing I know about Chris; it's that he likes to make new friends. He wants to be your friend. He wants to help you unlock your ideas because he knows, in turn, it will help unlock even more ideas for himself, just as it has with his friendship with me over the years. Life is a collaboration, but we have to be the ones to put our own personal projects into motion first. Once you break that inertia, you'll be surprised how many other cool people you start attracting out there to help perpetuate that motion.

You don't need to take Chris' advice. You don't need to take my advice. But I hope you do. Go ahead, turn the page.

Let this be the start of your next adventure.

Just go.

PART 1

STORIES

Chris Ruggiero

THE URGE TO JUST GO

It's inside every one of us because many of years of evolution have ingrained inside our DNA a voice shouting to keep moving. Keep moving or lions will eat you. Keep moving or you'll run out of food. Keep moving or you'll die. That's how most of the humans that ever existed lived their entire lives.

At first I thought about how terrible that must have been, then that feeling of complete freedom kicks in. Imagine being able to just pack up and move somewhere new whenever you needed to find something to eat. There is no house, no school, no society dictating what's 'normal.'

You just go.
Go wherever you want.
Go whenever you want.
And never come back.

Nearly every person I've ever talked to says they just want to travel and explore new places. Most of us don't have to outrun lions or hunt and gather food to survive, but the desire to keep moving will never go away.

Sometimes I start long drives at 3 AM. There's something about the darkness and desolation of the open roads. It's a cinematic scene playing in my mind and I'm the hero. There's no story except the one I'm about to create.

I'm free.
Maybe I'll go chase lions today.

Those early morning drives make me feel like I've been let in on the earth's best kept secrets. A head start on the day while everyone is still sleeping. A magical window is transporting me to a place to witness the sunrise in a whole new world.

When I have a day off from shows, I often find myself in strange places.

It was September 2012 and Kip had some time off so we hit the road. I had some shows, but there were a few days in between for us to just go.

"Have you ever been to Niagara Falls?"
"No."
"Yeah me neither. Wanna go now?"

It wasn't even a question. We were already on our way.

I hate touristy things, but feeling the power of that water hitting your face is a reminder of how amazing the world is. We didn't last long at the overlook you see in photos. We were off to explore. We hopped the no trespassing fence and all of the sudden we had a private tour of the entire waterfront upstream from the falls. Our own backstage pass to the world.

Looking back up to the busy trail filled with tourists is a reminder for me to never follow any rules ever. Why isn't everyone allowed to be down here to enjoy the real experience? They'll never know what they're missing.

There are rules so stupid people don't do stupid things. Stupid people don't like freedom. They like other people to tell them what to do.

Don't be stupid. Do what you want.

Just go.

COVER STORY

The photo on the cover is one of my favorite photos that's ever been taken of me. It's at Monument Valley in the middle of the desert in Utah. It's the exact spot that, 20 years prior, Forest Gump claimed, "...and just like that my running days was over."

Flash back to three days earlier. It's 5 am and I'm watching the airplane I'm supposed to be on unload all of my fellow passengers' luggage because the airplane is broken. It looked fine to me, but apparently I'm not qualified to make that call. Hearing that evil woman behind the speakers announcing the flight is canceled is the worst sound in the world.

Flash back to a few weeks before that. "Kip, want to meet me in Arizona in a couple weeks?"

If you offer up any type of impractical trip that has a slight potential of a good story, Kip will be there.

The plan was to meet in Albuquerque, NM by noon. We both had flights that would get us there about that time.

I had to call with the bad news conveyed to me by the demon behind the speaker. I call her that because I can't imagine her being an actual person. Real humans can't be this cruel.

But our plans for an adventure weren't about to get ruined by that static filled airport announcement.

"I'll find a way."

I always do.

Just go.

After a few buses and airplanes that weren't broken, I see the sandy landscape get closer and the plane touches down.

3 days with no plans. The world is ours. We made it. We're free. The endless desert void of vegetation spans

to the distant mountains on the horizon. Are we still on earth? This feels like a movie.

"Let's go to the Forest Gump place."
"How far are we from there?"
"About a 3 hour drive into Utah."
"OK, grab the camera."

So we drove. I'm often envious of the pioneers who got to explore and go on these adventures before anyone had ever seen them. That is until my iPhone stops working and there's no internet or GPS to guide our way. Imagine finding your way via a map made out of paper?

Imagine being the person who had to make the map!

It seems impossible. So many things are impossible until you do them. I didn't think we'd ever make it to the spot I saw in the movie.

But there's a picture to prove we made it.

We got there because we made one decision.

Just go.

HOW DID I GET HERE?

Lying in a hotel bed in some town you've never heard of, the silence is so loud it's hard to decipher even my own thoughts.

An hour earlier I was in a different universe. I was about to finish my show in front of a couple hundred college students. The unicycle that's taller than I am is being held by two college dudes with hoodies on to remind me of whatever college I'm at. I'm about to climb on and juggle to the crowd's delight.

When I hear stories of my heroes on stage they always talk about how you can't see the audience when on stage. That was a different time.

I look out to a sea of glowing faces as the Snapchat story they're recording for their friends who didn't come to the show seems more important than the real live performer in front of them. Sometimes I find myself falling into the same trap. Am I living this experience right now or just recording it like a zombie through a screen that I can show to strangers on the internet to prove how adventurous my life is?

"They're going to be so impressed. This video will be the one to go viral and make me a star," I keep telling myself.

I bet more people have seen me on that unicycle in Snapchat stories than have seen it in person. That might be an exaggeration but it feels true sometimes.

As the music kicks in, the crowd adds some noise with some cheers. A couple lone claps from the few without a phone in hand can be heard sometimes. I'm now juggling while balanced on a big pink unicycle. While there's only a couple hundred eyes on me here, the whole world is watching through their phone. Probably from the dorm room across campus, but still.

As I walk off stage I remind the audience I'm available after the show for pictures and to give out posters. If I was decently entertaining, there will be a small line of people who take me up on the offer. That's my favorite part of the entire day. I get to feel like a big star. Even though they've never heard of me an hour before, they're lined up to take photos.. with me! Jugglers don't ever actually get famous, but a few people wanting to meet after a show gives a nice taste of what it might be like.

After I pack up the show and walk out of the theater it all changes. I'm just back to being a face in the crowd. If you've never gone to a restaurant or bar alone, you should experience it. Your thoughts get the best of you as you wonder if you should go talk to a group of strangers.

"Maybe they'll come talk to me when they notice I'm alone," is something you'll wonder (it rarely happens).

Sometimes I'll still be wearing my slightly flamboyant stage outfit which will get the occasional mocking "Nice pants!" comment. I just laugh to myself and think about all the autographs I just signed.

Back in the hotel room I can reflect on all of this.

If I'm in the mood to complain about something there's plenty I could come up with, but I remember... I have the best job ever.

People pay me to travel around the world. In return I just have to make them smile for an hour with some silly tricks I learned when I was a kid.

As a shy kid growing up, I barely talked to anyone. I couldn't imagine getting in front of a group of people and talking let alone performing. Throughout high school I ended up spending a lot of time on stage, but it was hiding behind a drum set. I never had to talk and no one really pays much attention to the drummer. Those drums created a safe place for me. Like a barrier protecting me from the audience. I had a desire to ditch the drums and steal the show but the comfort of not taking that risk always won. I think often of all the things we miss out on because living a boring life inside our comfort zone seems better than risking failure and trying something new.

When looking at colleges to attend, Penn State caught my eye with their clubs run by students that gave you a home no matter what your weird hobby was. But I didn't get accepted.

A couple years of perfect grades at a smaller local school, East Stroudsburg University, proved I was capable of holding my own in the big leagues. Penn State accepted me as a transfer student, so I packed my bags.

The Penn State Juggling Club would be my new home. Within a year, I was president of the club figuring out ways to make everyone on campus know who we were.

Appearing on the cover of the student newspaper on campus, The Daily Collegian, gave me a small taste of people knowing who I was. It all goes away the next day when someone else claims their own fame for 15 minutes.

Our photo from the cover of
Penn State's Daily Collegian newspaper.

I think that's a big driving force for people who do creative things. You get a small taste of people accepting and embracing what you do early on. It's a feeling some people are never lucky enough to experience. The first time it happens is euphoric. Friends are congratulating you, strangers are emailing you, it's everything you've imagined and more. You think that's the new way of life. But the next day comes and it's back to business as usual. Except now you're on a mission to get back to that level. But this time it's got to be bigger and better. The photo needs to be bigger, the article needs to be longer. No one will be impressed if things stay the same. I need more fame, more emails coming in, more strangers recognizing me. This might not go away, or maybe it gets replaced with something else when we get old enough to realize that at the end of the day no one is really impressed and you've only been trying to impress yourself this whole time.

I can look back and remember all the amazing times the Penn State Juggling Club provided, but just to keep a balance, I have to also mention there were countless winter nights that I would walk the icy campus to find no one else showed up. I'd wait around in the gymnasium space we had rented for an hour then go back home defeated.

Didn't anyone see me on the newspaper cover yesterday?? Oh yeah, everyone forgot already.

But people did show up. Sometimes a lot of people showed up. But I wasn't content juggling with other students in a racquetball court with no windows. If it was nice out we could juggle outside on the HUB lawn where almost everyone on campus had to walk by.

Juggling was able to spark some curiosity but it couldn't capture the imaginations of people to keep them around. I wanted to create something that would make people forget they were on their way to class and stay and watch us instead. My approach to how I create shows to this day is influenced by those endless hours spent on the HUB lawn learning how to captivate audiences.

I'm not sure why, but for some reason jugglers often become friends with magicians. I'm quite lucky this is the case.

Maybe juggling and magic go so well together because juggling offers a great visual to grab people's attention instantly and magic captures some other mysterious part of people's attention to keep them intrigued. All I knew was that the student organization website had a listing for the Penn State Performing Magicians.

Kip and I had been working on a trick of our own. We only really cared about doing something cool to skip lines at bars and impress the girls once we got in. Turns out our trick was pretty good and even impressed the real magicians. We were in.

I organized the best jugglers and magicians into a super group of performers and called it the Out of Hand Variety Show. When calls came in from events looking for jugglers I offered them a juggling and magic variety show unlike anything they'd seen. I had no idea what I was doing, but I didn't worry about anything.

The first shows were mostly us performing to music and not talking. As we realized how boring that was, we started adding more talking parts with jokes and comedy skits. I didn't realize it at the time, but it was a training ground and a perfect experimental beginning to my One Man Variety Show that would soon bring me around the world.

The grass started to appear greener, as it always does, on the other side. I was soon ready to branch out and do my own shows. I loved performing with other people, but I was longing for the freedom to do whatever I wanted without relying on other performers or worrying about different styles of performing meshing well for audiences.

I started doing mostly kids' shows around the Penn State area and distinctly remember the feeling of how bad they were. I had no idea what people wanted to see and still was under the impression that people might care a little bit about the actual juggling.

With every show I did, I established a reason to WHY I was doing that particular juggling routine. People connect to a story, not the skills you possess.

Everyone has skills and no one cares about anything that everyone has.

Find a way to use the skills you possess to connect other people and you'll be on your way to something great.

FINE, I'LL DO IT MYSELF

Every one of us has dreams and goals we aren't doing anything about. As I did more shows, they got better with each performance but I had some voice in me telling me I was still an amateur. I didn't want to be an amateur but maybe I was falling back into a comfort zone that was too scary to leave. Am I good enough to call myself a pro? What if everyone finds out I'm just a fraud with no qualifications?

I'm thankful to now realize that no one has qualifications to do anything. Some people just jump in and do it and GET qualified. It never comes from anyone else. It's a change in mindset. It comes down to the classic idea of 'fake it 'til you make it.'

The next level for me was to perform at colleges. I saw performers visit Penn State when I was a student and I worshiped them. How cool that they get to travel around the country visiting college campuses and get paid to perform! I had to throw the amateur feelings out the window so I could join the big leagues.

I learned that most performers got booked through agencies. I wanted an agent. I looked up every agency that represented acts that performed at colleges and enthusastically sent them my promotional materials.

"They'll love that I'm a fresh performer on the scene with a new show," I thought.

But they didn't respond. Well some did, but they said no. No one accepted me. No one was willing to give me a chance, so I had to go out and do it myself. That's just what I was prepared to do.

Acts get booked at colleges through big booking conferences that take place across the country. My plan was to get invited to attend these expensive conferences by my new agent that I didn't have.

At this point I've learned this lesson over and over. If you want something done right, do it yourself. Times are changing though, so let's alter this. If you want something done at all, you've got to do it yourself.

No one cares about you. People only care about themselves. It's nothing personal, no matter how much it feels like it is.

Not a single agency was willing to help make my dream a reality. Why would they? What did I have to offer them? How can I make THEIR dream a reality? I wasn't thinking like this then, but I knew if I wanted to do it, I just had to do it.

Was I qualified?

Nope.

I went anyway. I did extensive research to prepare myself and spent all my money to attend my first conference. I booked one show that paid about half the amount I paid to be there. Success!

But the real success is never measured in the outcomes that you're looking for. For me, the real success was saying hello to someone I looked up to. Jonathan Jones from Waking Ashland and We Shot the Moon happened to be at this event. I had been a fan of his music for years and I noticed him hanging out the first night of the conference so I decided to say hello.

It turned out that he was running his own agency and they might be looking for additional acts. The following year, I attended 5 booking conferences under his agency. I was making waves and what seemed like overnight, I was getting emails from all the agencies that ignored me a year ago.

I was finally qualified. I just had to offer them something they wanted. They wanted someone who was willing to go out there and get it himself.

I got offers from all the top agencies to join their roster. I joined my top pick agent.

Once again, I thought this was my ticket. I find that happens a lot. I think, "If only I had this, then everything would work out."

"This" is always something different for all of us. More money, more opportunity, more youth, more experience, more motivation, more whatever. Here's a tip: if you aren't making it happen with what you've got, you won't make it happen with whatever 'more' you want.

The new agency was great, but wasn't a perfect fit for me so I left them to join a smaller agency.

I'm constantly reminded of these lessons:

- No one is going to make my dreams come true except me.
- Someone is envious of exactly the circumstances you have right now, so make the most of it.
- I'm not qualified (and neither is anyone else) until I go out and do it. No one cares if you're qualified or not. The only thing that matters is that you go do it. Whatever it is, stop thinking about it, stop talking about it and do it.

THE BIG LEAGUES

It was the beginning of 2012 and I went to sleep every night wondering if I'd get a 6AM call. I was a substitute teacher at Bangor High School, the same place I went to high school as a student a few years before.

I hated it.

As a student I remember thinking, "At least these teachers get paid to be here."

But now I WAS a teacher. I was getting paid to be there. As a substitute I didn't even really need to do anything except show up and take attendance. Sounds like a dream job.

I hated it even more.

Most of the students were awesome and knew as long

as no one got physically injured I didn't really care if they did their work or not. I was the best teacher EVER.

Ever notice that whenever you give a group of people something awesome, one of them insists on ruining it for everyone? Every classroom I walked into had one idiotic student who thought it was his or her job to make my life hell.

I could write an entire book about the horrors of being a substitute teacher, but that's not the point here.

It was a catch 22 when the phone rang each morning. An off-balance scale of being partly excited to make some cash mixed with a crippling anxiety of the horrors that these monsters had in store for me.

But sometimes all it takes is one unexpected phone call to turn things around. One evening the phone rang from a strange number. I hate answering unknown calls so it went to voicemail.

As I listened to this magical message I felt everything start to change. It wasn't gradual. It all changed instantly.

The call was from Armed Forces Entertainment asking

me if I'd like to go to an island in the middle of the Indian Ocean to spread smiles to the troops stationed there with my juggling show.

YES.

Why don't calls like that come every day instead of those terrible substitute teacher calls?

Did I forget to mention that in addition to my juggling show, the tour will be with six NFL cheerleaders?

I never did tell the sub caller that I wouldn't be available for the next few weeks. I have to assume she cheered in excitement of me escaping when she heard my voicemail greeting informing callers that I had left the country to have the BEST TIME OF MY LIFE.

There were late night adventures in Singapore that justified the $37 drinks. If you ever want to feel really awesome about life, go out on the town in a different country with a crew of professional cheerleaders. I'm not a famous person, but I'm sure that's what it feels like.

I was gone for a few weeks to perform for the troops for about an hour throughout a few days. The rest of the time was spent hanging out at the beach, sailing, barbecuing, and exploring the island of Diego Garcia.

We hung out in the airport control tower, got behind the scenes tours of the ships that carry gear and live ammo into combat zones and sat in helicopters that were being shot at days earlier. Whenever I get frustrated about anything, I remember how thankful I am that I don't have to fly one of those things while getting shot at. Huge props to everyone who actually does that.

It was like opening the door to a fantasy land where everything was perfect, but as our time on the island ran out, I found myself wishing it could last forever. How can I make this feeling never end?

I never answered the sub caller's phone calls ever again.

This trip was full of moments I had to keep checking to make sure I wasn't dreaming.

Learning some new tricks.

Welcomed to the island by the best.

No caption necessary.

Chris Ruggiero

PART 2

PHOTOS

Chris Ruggiero

Where it all started.
Penn State Juggling Club.

Probably entertaining strangers at our house in State College.

Not a boy band.
The crew I assembled at Penn State
to create Out of Hand Entertainment

Making my own clothing long before the ideas of
Between Dreams were born.

Desperately trying to look cool in promo photo origins. Luckily I quickly learned that it's impossible to look coool while juggling in photos.

*Random photo shoots on campus
(trying-to-look-cool theme going strong).*

I think this was my first "proper" promo photo for my solo show. Special shoutout to Photoshop.

One time, I flew to the Cayman Islands to surprise Kip for
his birthday while he was in vet school.
Why wouldn't we take a photo like this?

Performing for a big crowd on the street.

*When you live with the "just go" attitude, really
cool things happen.
Flying airplanes with my friend, Joey.*

Parking lot skate sessions in who knows what state.

The cast of The Curious Show in
Atlantic City in our "dressing room."

Enjoying the sunshine in the middle of the Indian Ocean.

*Warming up the crowd for the headliners at
the Glamour Kills shows... with juggling.
Lots of confused faces in the crowd.*

Learning how to street perform at Musikfest in Bethlehem, PA. The only way to learn was to jump in and go!

More from Musikfest. Performing for the big crowds with my brother, Mike.

Sound checking on the big stage at NACA.
I believe this was Spokane, WA.

Photoshoot idea, wisely rejected.

Slipper Room has been my home in NYC. A place to explore and experiment on stage with complete creative freedom to do whatever you want. A dream venue I'm lucky to be part of.

Sometimes the stage lights make me nervous, but mostly they're a comforting sight to remind me how lucky I am to share my creations with the world.

Sometimes resting "backstage" before the show means sitting on the floor of a gymnasium. I'll add that some of the least glamorous shows are the most rewarding.

Interesting costume choices while performing in NYC.

About to juggle fire on a ball at the Burlesque Show at Borgata in Atlantic City. Spending a few months performing in this show was one of my favorite things I've ever done.

Hiding from the noisy casino at my favorite quiet spot on top of the parking deck at Borgata.

Down time in Atlantic City always meant going out to explore and take photos. Apparently sitting down was my go-to pose.

Hanging out in the girls' dressing room backstage before the show for some reason.

Warming up on stage before 1,000 people fill those seats.

Hanging out with cast members.

Probably making it sound like what I'm about to do is way harder than it actually is.

More time off in Atlantic City.
More taking photos.
More sitting.

On stage at Borgata.

Celebrating the New Year in Atlantic City with some friends.

Exploring the world one city at a time.
Skateboarding under the Pittsburgh skyline.

Exploring Los Angeles.

The latest promo.

PART 3

YOUR

TURN

Chris Ruggiero

WHY BEING BAD AT THINGS IS AWESOME

I see people doing cool stuff all the time and wish I could be like them. I don't want to spend the time they put into learning how to do it. I just want to be good at it right now.

They say with 10 thousand hours of practice you can be an expert at anything. I dont know if that's true, but I imagine if I spent 5 hours every day for 5 years I'd be pretty good at almost anything.

What does being an expert even mean? Is there some day when you wake up and can claim that title? Do you slowly progress toward it? Are you ever really an expert at anything?

I want to be an expert at lots of things... I want to be an expert entertainer, but I also want to be an expert video creator, podcast host, blog writer, friend, person.

How perfect is the world that we can't wake up and just be great at what we want? Think about living in that world. You have an idea and you're instantly amazing at it! But what happens next? There's no where to go but down. That's not a world I'm willing to accept. Sounds like constant disappointment as your dreams slowly crumble away as you pursue them.

The world we live in is perfect.

You can chase any dream you want, but when you start you're really going to suck.. for a long time. This weeds out the losers. Losers put an effort for a few months and don't see immediate results, so they quit.

I want to win. But to win you have to be willing to be really bad at things. Being bad is an awesome feeling because it's the only way to push yourself to learn new things and get closer to being an expert. If you're living within your comfort zone, nothing awesome will be coming your way any time soon. That stuff is hiding somewhere else. But it's waiting for you. It's waiting for an expert. Someone to win. Someone to claim that prize.

Are you a winner? Better get started.

HOW FAR ARE YOU WILLING TO GO?

Those thoughts in your mind that come up with excuses are not based on reality. They are based on fear. The more fuel you feed them, the more logical and real they become. Excuses are crutches you create to make yourself feel better about not taking action.

It's easier for you to admit why you can't do something than to actually try it and risk failure.

We have excuses for everything. Not exercising, eating bad food, making stupid decisions, but you must always remember these excuses are nothing except decisions that we chose. When you find yourself making an excuse, think of it another way. Think of it as a crossroads. One direction leads to nothing except your excuse and the other leads to actually doing and succeeding.

The first step toward excuses is easy but there's a never-ending mountain of more challenges and disappointments to live with.

The first steps... no, miles of making the decision to follow your dreams are not easy. But you will hit a point where it's no longer an uphill battle. It requires no more effort to live a life of abundance and prosperity than a life of wanting and wishing. It's time to choose what you want.

If you want a life full of what you have now, keep doing what you're doing. But you want more. So what are you willing to do about it?

> "*I bargained with Life for a penny,*
> *And Life would pay no more,*
> *However I begged at evening*
> *When I counted my scanty store.*
>
> *For Life is just an employer,*
> *He gives you what you ask,*
> *But once you have set the wages,*
> *Why, you must bear the task.*
>
> *I worked for a menial's hire,*
> *Only to learn, dismayed,*
> *That any wage I had asked of Life,*
> *Life would have willingly paid.*"
> -Jessie B. Rittenhouse

ASKING FOR PERMISSION IS ASKING FOR REJECTION

We're living in the most exciting time in the history of the world. I was just working on a project in photoshop and had no idea what I was doing. Within 30 seconds after a google search, I had my solution.

I have instant access to everything every human has ever learned. More importantly, we have access to connect with anyone in the world. As an entertainer this is the most exciting thing for me. There are millions of people at this second scouring their computers for fresh entertainment. Consuming content faster than ever.

Not very long ago, if you wanted to entertain people in any sense you had to wait for someone's permission. Whether you were an actor trying to make it in hollywood or a musician trying to get a record deal, that was the only way for you to reach the masses. Those days are long gone. The biggest stars today are people creating their own fan base.

What do you have that you'd like to share with the world? You've got a computer to post a blog, you've got a piece of plastic in your pocket that has more technology than we had when we went to the moon and you're playing Candy Crush.

No one's going to give you permission to do anything. And if you do ask, they'll probably say no anyway.

What are you going to do today that someone said you couldn't do?

COLLABORATION, NOT COMPETITION WILL MAKE YOU AWESOME

Competition exists everywhere. In one way it encourages every living creature to be its best in order to survive. Trees growing in a forest must compete to grow tall in order to reach the sunlight to stay alive.

But if you think about what the trees are doing, it's helping each and every one to grow strong and tall. One tree isn't sabotaging another in order to get more sunlight. They aren't reaching out and pushing others over.

For some reason that's what some people do. They understand that competition is necessary for everyone to grow and improve, but they take it to the point of harming others so they can triumph.

But what happens next? If you shut the other person

down and you 'win' where are you left? It might look like you're at the top, and maybe you are. But now you've eliminated competition at your level. Sounds awesome except now a whole new breed of competition is coming up together to take your crown. You won't be developing new skills to tackle new problems that arise because it looks like no one can touch you.

They're coming for you.

They are competing for your title, but not in the way you did it. They are collaborating. Encouraging each other to fight and grow tall.

In the forest, there is no winner. No emperor that wins the battle to be the best tree. That would be a pretty lame looking forest and no one would be impressed by that one tree.

Look at the trees, they are all surviving. All growing tall. All working together to create an amazing forest.

When we look at competition as a collaboration we build each other up rather than tear each other down and we can create something larger than any one person can comprehend.

Let's be like the trees. Let's build a forest together.

IT'S KIND OF FUN TO DO
THE IMPOSSIBLE

Standing under Mount Rushmore looking at those faces carved into the side of the mountain towering hundreds of feet above me had me speechless. Creating something of this magnitude is beyond my comprehension, but it all started with one person's idea. An idea that once acted upon, faced more complications and troubles than you could imagine.

But there it is. It happened. An idea that will be immortalized for hundreds or thousands of years.

Guglielmo Marconi is credited as the inventor of radio transmission, but he was forced into a mental hospital when he announced he discovered a way to send messages through the air without wires.

The best ideas are so incredible that people around you will say they are impossible. That's how you know they're good.

"It's kind of fun to do the impossible."
-Walt Disney

BE NICE AND COOL THINGS HAPPEN. A GUIDE TO TRAVELING THE WORLD

"You're so lucky you get to travel and get paid for it," is a thing I hear most people say to me when I talk about being on the road doing shows.

Sometimes I need to be reminded how awesome it is to be able to travel and never have to do the same thing every day. Traveling can be the most stressful thing in the world, but no matter what happens, there's always an opportunity to spin it into an awesome learning experience. Travel forces you to look for the positives in every situation. I guess you could focus on the bad parts. If you want to be miserable and are looking for the negatives you won't have a hard time finding them.

Your brain has a funny way of finding exactly what it's

looking for.

I'm looking for a good time, but I have to remind myself often to eliminate the poisonous thoughts. Jealousy, anger, frustration will all ruin your day.

Things won't work out how you expect. And that's pretty cool. You'll have to adapt to canceled flights, lost hotel reservations, getting stuck in endless traffic, and countless other unexpected issues. Each one offers an opportunity to experience something awesome that you might not have been able to do if your plans got in the way.

People are nice and strangers can become friends very quickly if you're open to stepping out of your comfort zone

I got stuck in Rapid City, SD for an extra day that I wasn't expecting or prepared for. The girl at the front desk is usually the person you take your frustrations out on. They have nothing to do with the problem and probably can't do anything about it, but we just want to be angry at someone.

If I've learned anything from travel, it's this; be nice to people who have access to the computer that can get you things you need (re-booked flights, last minute hotel rooms, rental cars). I was nice and chatted about my issue which led to her giving me a ride to return my car (which I didn't want to pay an extra day for) and got a nice 'buddy discount' on the hotel room for the next night.. oh and upgraded to a suite and even a dinner friend later that day.

If you find yourself in Rapid City soon, go be nice to someone working at the Hotel Alex Johnson.

Here's the lesson: be nice and cool things happen to you.

Whether you travel the world, or go to work each day, we're all traveling through life. Each day passes faster than the last.

Appreciate the small moments.

As a traveler you're always leaving soon, so let's do this together and make the most of right now.

YOU PROBABLY DON'T SUCK AS MUCH AS YOU THINK YOU DO

Nearly every time I get off stage, I think about what I could have done better and focus on the things that didn't go perfectly. I beat myself up because I want it to be perfect. Sometimes even half way through a show, I'll notice that the crowd might be a little bit quiet or not as enthusiastic as I'd like.

I've talked to almost all of my entertainer friends about this and everyone goes through it. We want our show to be the best it can be. Some nights everything works. There's a great crowd, all of our routines are working, there's not technical issues happening behind the scenes, everything is perfect.

Those nights spoil you. You start to expect that to be the normal. It's not. Most of the time, things aren't perfect.

Sometimes the sound system stops working.

Sometimes you're performing in a cafeteria and the smoothie blender picks the worst times to interrupt the show.

Sometimes you drove 12 hours to the show and you're tired.

Sometimes the ceiling height is inches above your head and you're trying to do a juggling show.

Chances are you're not an entertainer, so you haven't had these problems. But you've had some issues in whatever you do when the situation is less than ideal.

You can't do much about the actual situation, but you can decide how you'll react to it. Since perception is reality, you can change the reality of the situation by changing how you're looking at it and how you're thinking about it.

I've had plenty of shows where I wasn't especially happy about my performance when I walked off stage.

Luckily there's always a reminder that I need to change my perception of the show. It's easy to forget that the people that come to my show have never seen anything like this before. They are so excited to see what I do up close and in person.

I've never done a show where people haven't come up to me when I finish and thank me for coming to perform for them. Sometimes it's a huge line of people wanting photos with me. Many times it's only a handful of people, but never zero.

After a recent show, a girl was so excited she told me all of her favorite parts of the show and how much she absolutely loved it, then gave me a hug.

No matter what you're doing, there's a few people who are admiring you, thankful for what you're offering to the world. They might not be waiting for you after work to get your autograph, but trust that they're there. You're making a difference and people appreciate that. When things are tough remember that someone is counting on you.

I'm counting on you.

Don't let me down.

REJECTION SUCKS...
SO YOU HAVE TO BE BETTER

We want things to go in our favor, especially when we put ourselves out there and take risks. Any time we do something that could be great, we face the risk of rejection. It doesn't matter what it is, from a romantic interest to a job promotion, it's not fun when anyone tells you no.

There's a persistent illusion that tells us we want to be accepted for who we are, how we are at this moment.

I'm so glad that illusion isn't real. I want a lot of people to tell me no. I want to know what I'm not good at.

If no one ever told me no, I'd still be doing a crappy show thinking it was awesome.

I decided to create my own juggling variety show and

make a living touring the world. If you can imagine how much rejection I've faced multiply that by a big number and it might be a bit closer to the real number.

TONS of people have told me NO.

No, we don't have a good fit for a show like yours on our agency's roster.
No, your show isn't a good fit for our venue.
No.

(Silence) An unreturned email is the worst kind of NO. Not even a reason, just nothing.

No, you're not good enough.

Sometimes the no comes from yourself.

Time to send more emails.
That won't work. It's time to send BETTER emails. Make better phone calls. Create a better show.

BE BETTER.

EVERYDAY, BE A BETTER _____.

Pick something to fill in the blank and be better at it

today than you were yesterday. Maybe that's just being a better person. Yeah, that's what everyone should put in that space.

Be a better person. If you haven't started yet, now's the time.

Get ready for rejection. Lots of it. Use it to be better. Use it to be the best. Maybe you'll start hearing a new three letter word.

ARE YOU PUSHING THE LIMITS OR ARE YOU PLAYING IT SAFE?

Almost every piece of information I can find on body language talks about how to improve how you come across to other people. This is clearly an important aspect of taking control of your own body language, but they are missing out on a key concept. Body language is vital in influencing YOURSELF.

I have been focusing lately on pushing the limits of what I'm capable of. I'm closing the gap between my current state and my unlimited potential.

Yes, UNLIMITED potential. That's what we all have. It's waiting to be activated. Waiting for you to take control of your life to see how far you can push the limits. How do you know how far you can go unless you start pushing those limits?

"I want to stand as close to the edge as I can without going over." - Kurt Vonnegut

It's a fascinating idea, but I'm not interested in standing on the edge. I want to leap off and fly. I want to see that edge disappear on the horizon as I soar away.

"The Edge... there is no honest way to explain it because the only people who really know where it is are the ones who have gone over." -Hunter S. Thompson

That's more like it.

Are you pushing the limits or are you accepting what other people say is possible? Have they gone to the edge? How do they know what *you're* capable of? The only reason anyone is telling you what you can or can't do is because they are attempting to hold you back.

I bet they can't even fly.

And they wouldn't know if they could because they've never even gone close to the edge.

I thought this was going to be about body language and I think it still is, but I'm not going to tell you to improve your body language in order to impress other people. Use body language to trick yourself into feeling confident. Stand tall and smile. The smile comes from the inside. You don't have to do anything with your face.

Every time you walk through a doorway, imagine you're about to save the world. You can't let them down. They believe you're their hero. Do you believe too? I want to save the world with you. I believe.

So keep pushing the limits. Keep saving the world.

Keep flying.

I'm right behind you. Let's take the leap together.

Preparing for flight on the edge of an 800 foot cliff. Spider Rock at Canyon De Chelly, Arizona.

CALL YOURSELF AN EXPERT BECAUSE MAYBE YOU ARE

How many people label themselves as an "aspiring" _____? There are plenty of words to fill in.

Dancer, singer, musician, writer, film maker...

For some reason people pursuing creative things often label themselves as aspiring. I don't know why anyone would willingly call themselves an amateur at anything. You either are or you aren't. Do or do not, there is no try.

It sounds like an excuse to me. An 'out' for when you don't find success you can say, "Well at least I tried. It was only a hobby anyway."

You say those things so it's easier to accept failure.

Are truly great creative people aspiring to be anything? Sure, maybe they have aspirations, but there's no reason to label yourself as a crappy version of whatever you're doing.

I want to be an expert at a lot of things.

I want to be an expert writer. And I write things now. Am I an aspiring writer? Yeah some might say so, but I call myself a writer.

I write, so I'm a writer. If I would add *aspiring* to that I'd feel like I wasn't any good. Maybe I'm not any good, but for me to share this with the world, I have to believe that this is good and might help someone or at least entertain them. If I'm only aspiring to do anything I've already accepted that I'm no good and it probably won't work.

I'm going to start calling myself an expert at everything I WANT to be an expert at. I don't know if anyone will believe me but I don't care about them. I want to be the best for me, not for them.

Don't strive to be better than other people. Stop aspiring to do anything. Just do the thing. Believe you're the best.

Maybe you are.

YOUR DREAMS WILL NEVER COME TRUE. HERE'S WHY YOU NEED TO KEEP DREAMING ANYWAY.

Ever wonder what would happen if all your dreams came true? Don't worry, it'll never happen. I'm not saying you won't accomplish awesome things. You got this.

But isn't there some saying about as you approach the horizon it just keeps getting further away?

That's what happens to your dreams and goals. That place you're trying to get to is reachable. It's a lot closer than you think. But as soon as you approach, something shiny and new appears on a new distant horizon. Calling your name, tempting you to go further. Maybe it's comfortable right where you are. Maybe you're happy that you've accomplished all that you have. But I bet you can't resist that frontier. It's almost mocking you.

"I bet you can't catch me."

Don't tell me I can't do something.

I can do anything. I can do everything.

Well I can't do everything yet. But I'm trying. I'm learning. I'm running as fast as I can to that horizon, but it's running even faster. I need to learn how to run faster. Maybe it's not about running, but figuring out a way to move faster with less effort. I think that's what learning is. That's what wisdom is. There's no shortcut to wisdom. You can't read about it. You can't learn it. You need to live it. I want to live.

Life is a big high speed chase. You're either part of it or you're watching it on the big screen.

You're either chasing or being chased.

You get to pick.

Lead or follow.

I want to lead. I'm a leader. I don't want to learn someone else's lessons. I don't want anyone else's wisdom. I'm searching the ever expanding frontier for something I'm not sure exists. Maybe I'll know it when I see it or maybe it will never be.

It's not about finding anything. It's about searching.

Maybe the horizon will keep getting further away. I sure hope so.

I never want to arrive.

Keep going. If you're chasing, start leading. Make something so incredible that someone will chase you. Keep going until you're done.

And know this for sure. You'll never be done.

I took this photo in the middle of the Indian Ocean.
Somewhere I never imagined I'd ever be. My dreams get
bigger by the minute. I hope yours do too.
If you keep following the horizon, you'll end up in amazing
places you never even knew existed.

BEGGARS CAN'T BE WINNERS

That's not how the saying goes. But I like it this way better.

Everyone's had a time when someone said, "Beggars can't be choosers." I guess it's a way of saying you should be grateful for what other people are doing for you.

No one wants to be a beggar or to have to rely on others for anything. We want to be self-sufficient. I imagine it's some sort of instinctual thing that we strive to be in power.

I want to be able to offer something valuable to people every day. I don't know the way to do this, so I try to do a lot of things. Maybe someone will connect with something I create and be inspired to create something of their own. If I do enough live shows, write enough blog posts, create enough podcasts and post enough videos maybe 1 out of 10 will be good. Those numbers suck but I'm ok with it.

A lot of people believe everything they touch is gold and they are amazing. That's not me. I know everything I do isn't going to change lives but 10% of what I do might. Maybe it's even only 1%.

That just means I better keep creating a lot of things. Maybe I'll get better and that number will change to 20% or 50%. It'll never be 100%. I'm thankful for that. It's the failures that make the successes so exciting.

When I posted an essay about rejection and striving to be better on my blog it quickly became my most successfull post. This was due to a handful of Facebook friends sharing it. The best feeling ever is to see people enjoy something you've created so much that they take the effort to share it with all their friends.

But the next day something surprised me. I THOUGHT I'd be inspired to write another post that people will love.

I then realized that the next post probably won't be so well received. I wanted to take in another day of glory from that post instead of posting something that might not be as amazing.

I wanted to share it again and beg more people to click it. It would extend my illusion of winning for one more day.

That's not how it works. I have to keep creating. I need to work through my next 9 posts to find the next gem. Maybe it won't be 9, maybe it'll be 20. Or maybe the next one will be killer. When I hit the submit button, I have no idea what will happen.

I only know what will happen if I don't hit the button. No one will read. No one will share. No one will care.

I want people to read. I want people to share. I want people to be inspired. I want to inspire people to create something that inspires me. It's a circle where everyone wins. We can win together. They say it's lonely at the top, but that's only if you're there by yourself. I'm on my way and I'm bringing all of you with me.

I want to win. I want you to win. No one needs to lose. Losers lose. We're not losers. We're winners.
Stop begging.
Start choosing.
Let's keep creating.
Let's keep winning.

STARS CAN'T SHINE WITHOUT DARKNESS

What? That's not true at all.

What we perceive as darkness has nothing to do with a star's shine. Those stars don't care if we happen to be on the dark side of the earth at the moment. The stars aren't shining for us to see. They are blazing away just as brightly and furiously all day and night.

We can take a lesson from them by not doing amazing things for the recognition or praise. Sure the stars are a great bonus to make our nights beautiful, but without us to appreciate them, they still burn.

I always want to claim credit for things I accomplish or help others to accomplish. I need to remind myself to allow them to have the entire spotlight they deserve without trying to steal some for myself.

I'm reminded of the words of the Tao Te Ching:

"The great leader works without self interest and leaves no trace.
When all is finished, the people say,
"We did it ourselves."

Here's a cheesy quote that's actually useful:

"Even after all this time
The sun never says to the Earth,
"You owe me."

Look what happens with a love like that,
It lights the whole sky."
- Hafiz

Who cares if no one's watching?

You're not doing it for them.

Keep burning.

ANOTHER STUPID QUOTE: NO EXPECTATIONS, NO DISAPPOINTMENTS

We've got so many options to do whatever we want and meet whoever we want. It's easy to say, "I'm going to set my expectations to zero so I'll never get let down. If this experience sucks, it's ok because I'll have plenty more opportunities."

It's true, that's a great way to never get let down.

It's also a great way to never have anything amazing happen.

Our brains are programmed to create a reality out of whatever we're imagining or expecting. It's why you consistently hear about world class athletes picturing success before competing. Extreme athletes (skateboarders, bikers, etc) play a movie in their mind of exactly what they are aiming to accomplish before their event.

Your subconscious mind can't tell the difference between imaginary scenarios and reality. It watches that movie and assumes it's reality and that it's possible. Once your subconscious mind accepts something as possible, there's no stopping it from becoming reality.

Whatever you set your expectations to is what you will get.

I heard Disney employees go through training that tells them to set their expectations as high as they can and consistently exceed them by 1%.

If we continue to set our expectations at a high level, great work will be what naturally happens. It won't be an uncommon event or a fluke.

Our natural state is one of curiosity and exploration. A state of believing that anything is possible. Think back to when you were 4. You truly believed that you could do anything. Over time older people convinced you that you were limited by something. Some force of nature will limit you and make certain things impossible. They stopped believing anything is possible so they think it's their job to convince you of the same.

"The moment you doubt whether you can fly, you cease forever to be able to do it." -Peter Pan

I have a specific goal that I'm working toward every day. It's a goal of making a certain amount of money. (I have plenty of other goals that don't have to do with money, don't worry).

You can make your own number and play along. I'm going to make this many dollars every week in a way that's enjoyable for myself and impacts others along the way.

I've mentioned this to a few people of varying ages and I consistently get responses like, "Well you better start playing the lottery" and "Yeah, wouldn't that be nice!"

YES, it would be nice. And it WILL be nice but I don't need to win the lottery. These people are stuck in some sort of poisonous thinking that says it's impossible to make a lot of money doing something they actually enjoy. Maybe they tried and failed, or maybe they were afraid to try, so they failed by default. Maybe some stupid adult told them it's not worth following their passion. It's better to chase the security of a 'real job.'

Maybe it was an innocent comment to keep the conversation going, or maybe it was an automatic response because they don't know how else to respond. If it wasn't helpful and supportive you need to eliminate that from your mindset at any cost. Maybe you need to stop being with people who have small thoughts. You can try to change people, but that rarely works.

Your brain has a capacity for a certain amount of activity. Every day I have to focus on filling it with positive things that are bringing me closer to accomplishing what I need to accomplish. Bad thoughts creep in constantly. We can't pretend they don't exist. I don't know how to eliminate them completely, but I can acknowledge they are there and instantly and consciously replace them with something useful.

I don't think this process ever ends, but rather becomes more automatic as we force it to become habit.

If you never want to be let down, never have expectations.

If you want to have an awesome life, have massively huge expectations and exceed them everyday.

WHAT HAPPENS WHEN NO ONE SHOWS UP?

Sometimes I wonder what would happen if I had a show and no one showed up. I got dangerously close to finding out at a recent show. A handful of people did show up... about 15. The room was set, ready for 200+ people to show up. If you build it, sometimes they won't come, so I was left with two options

1. Be upset about having a small crowd. I could have probably found someone to lay the blame on. The venue for not promoting well enough, the timing of the show coinciding with finals week at the college, the snapchat generation for not appreciating live entertainment, ME for not being able to draw a crowd.

2. Adapt the show and create an amazing and memorable night for the people that did show up. Forget about the excuses. Use that energy to have a great night.

When things aren't perfect I have to remind myself often that my job isn't to keep myself happy. I get paid to show up and make other people happy for an hour. When I get hired to perform at colleges I need to get the students to relax and forget about the stress of school work, studying, and whatever else they're going through that day. I'm lucky that I don't have to rely on ticket sales to make a living. It doesn't matter how many kids show up to my performance. I have a job to do for them. It doesn't matter if it's 1 person or 1,000.

If I give an ounce of my energy to being upset about the size of the crowd it would take away from the experience of each person that actually did show up. They deserve even more positive attention and energy when there's a small crowd.

A small crowd just makes me feel a little uneasy sometimes. It has something to do with seeing every person as an individual rather than as a 'crowd.' It's easy to win over a crowd, but with individuals it seems like you have to get them on your side one by one.

A few minutes into the show I felt great. I had to switch my mindset from a big stage show to just hanging out with some new friends that came out to see something cool. I abandoned my normal show and some of the routines I normally do and just went with the flow of what they wanted to see.

I stopped thinking about what would make me happy (a sellout show) and focused on making my audience happy. That's my job… my only duty.

I ended up having a great time performing this show. Almost everyone stayed after the show to talk to me.

If you've ever come to one of my shows, read a blog, watched a video or been involved in ANYTHING I've done, thank you. I'm learning to appreciate you as an individual, not just a part of the crowd.

This was the crowd minutes before walking onto stage.

WHY I DON'T BELIEVE IN NEW YEARS RESOLUTIONS

Have you ever followed through on a New Year's Resolution? Do you have the same one every year? 85% of New Year's Resolutions fail by Valentine's Day. I just made that up, but I bet it's pretty close to being true.

We LOVE the idea of a fresh start.

This year will be the year I change. This year I will live how I want to live.

But of course I'm not going to start today. I'm going to keep eating candy bars and sit on my ass all day until January 1st. I never need to do anything TODAY because I can always start TOMORROW. What will one day really hurt?

We don't really want to change our behaviors. We want

to imagine how great life would be if we changed. It's a much better fantasy to live than going through the pain of actually making a change.

What will your resolution be this coming year?

Why don't you start doing that today? Right now. If you can't start right now, what makes you think you'll start on the 1st?

New Year's Resolutions are stupid.

Not because I don't think improvement is important, but because resolutions never work. You need a lifestyle resolution.

Don't begin the New Year as a fresh start.

Begin today as a fresh start for the rest of your life.

Make a New Year's Resolution if you want to change for a month or two, but if you want to change what your life looks like, you've got to make those decisions every day.

This year, my New Year's Resolution is to wake up every day and have a "New Day Resolution."

I'm not going to start something next year.

I'm starting today.

I'm starting now.

And I'm going to have to start over tomorrow.

I'm going to have to start over every moment of every day.

I know I can't make a decision of how the next year will go, but I CAN make a decision of how this moment right now will go.

This moment is awesome.

Something might happen soon that won't be awesome, so I better keep enjoying and appreciating right now.

Maybe if I keep making awesome moments right now, they'll add up to an awesome year.

That's my resolution. Are you with me?

PEOPLE DON'T KNOW WHAT THEY'RE TALKING ABOUT. STOP LISTENING TO THEIR DUMB ADVICE.

That might be a funny thing to say when giving advice, to not listen to anyone's advice. But you can listen to me. I know what I'm talking about. Everyone says that, so maybe don't listen to me either.

People are idiots. They don't know what's best for you. No one is qualified to tell you what to do. I'm surely not.

You don't need to listen to me, but you're here so I assume you care what I'm saying.

I recently saw someone posting advice on "how to smile." As in, physically how to make your face smile.

WHO ARE YOU TO TELL ME HOW TO BE HAPPY?

It's in caps because I'm yelling.

He said you rest your upper teeth on your lower lip. Seriously, he told us how to smile. Am I taking crazy pills or is this insane?

Try it, look in the mirror. You look like as much of an idiot as that guy who posted that 'tip.'

Have you ever actually smiled naturally and done that? NO, you haven't, so why would you want to learn how to fake a smile?

Here's advice you CAN listen to. I'll teach you how to smile so you look better in photos.

The trick to smiling and looking good in photos and in real life (the trick to looking happy) is... BE HAPPY.

Happy people smile. Naturally.

Babies smile and laugh when they're happy. Everyone loves a smiling baby. Why do they look so cute? Because it's natural. They aren't worrying about how they look. They aren't worried about people judging them. They are just happy and they know it. And they really want to show it.

The point is people are desperate for clicks on their blog, so they post stuff they think is helpful but they're too dumb to realize how terrible they are (and how miserable their advice is).

Think twice before you take advice from someone writing a blog (or a book). Especially me.

But keep smiling... and do it however you want.

Smiling on stage and I'm doing it just fine.

EVERYONE KEEPS QUITING BECAUSE THEY'RE LOSERS. DON'T BE A LOSER.

The New York Times released an article saying more than 95% of blogs are abandoned. Sometimes I make up statistics, but I didn't make this up.

Why do so many people start things and give up? Maybe you're not into blogging, but we all have many things we started doing with a whole lot of enthusiasm then quit right when it started to get difficult. It's so easy to look at the people who are already successful and say, "I could do that."

No you can't.

Well you could. But you're not.

You keep giving up and complaining.

Why did they 'make it' while I'm still here envious of their success?

Because they didn't quit.

They were excited, so they started. It sucked, but they kept going. Something cool happened and there was a boost of enthusiasm. Then it sucked again. Then something cool happened again.

No one is doing everything awesome. The key is to keep going. Keep going when things are awesome and keep going when things are terrible.

Actually do MORE when things are terrible.

Everything you make WON'T be terrible, I promise. So if you're not producing your best, keep making stuff so a gem can emerge. It's a simple numbers game. The more stuff you do and create, the more garbage you create. But within that garbage there's hidden treasures.

It's not about creating awesome things. It's about creating *things*. The awesome will come, but you haven't earned it yet. You'll never earn it, so you'll have to keep creating... forever. You'll never reach the point where you say, "Cool, I'm good enough now, so I'll just hang out."

I guess some people do say that. Losers say that. Quitters say that.

But not me. Not you. We create garbage. Every day, more garbage.

Every day a potential to create something awesome is hiding, but the more you look for it, the deeper it goes. The only way to find it is through doing more work, creating more things.

Circus skills have a pesky way of constantly reminding me how much I suck at things. It would be really easy to quit all the time, but I keep going because I'm not a loser.

Here are some thoughts:

- Someone has been waiting for what you have to offer. Keep going long enough to find each other.

- Fail and do it quickly. Everyone sucks at first.. then almost everyone stops. You don't start out being good at anything. You get good by being bad for a long time.

- Spin everything that happens to you into a positive. Take lessons from every failure. People that seek positives find more positives. It's a way of literally increasing your luckiness.

- Rejection is only redirection. You were off path. Rejection is helping you get back on your path. You're moving onto something bigger and better.

- You'll never be perfect, but you can be better. Don't worry about where your final destination is. No one knows. Think about how tomorrow can be better than today. Your destination will be your journey.

- Keep creating. People are watching. People are waiting.

LET'S STOP TALKING OURSELVES OUT OF CREATING THINGS THE WORLD NEEDS

I was talking to my friend about having the confidence to walk on stage in front a crowd of strangers. It's an interesting thing with most people, not just entertainers - that from the outside, what we're doing looks like we're being brave and courageous, but on the inside we are often full of insecurities and self-doubt.

Most people know they aren't living up to their full potential, and while that can be encouraging and inspiring, it can also put a hurting on your self-esteem (but only if you allow it to).

I'm always working to improve my performances because I know I can learn from each show and make the next one better, but sometimes it becomes an obsession and I have to remind myself that sometimes good enough really is good enough.

I remember having an elementary school art teacher who's motto was "Good enough is not good enough."

See, she was planting in our little brains that things have to be perfect. That we need to keep putting more work in until it's just right.

I wish I was smarter back then to realize how wrong she was. Art is not perfect. Art will never be perfect. It's often the case that the more work and effort you put in actually makes it worse.

It might be better to let things go with the flow and see what happens.

This doesn't mean we should be lazy and wait for things to happen. Quite the opposite. We need to be hustling everyday, creating new things, sharing new ideas.

Everyone is full of good ideas, but good ideas are worthless until you do something with them. Then they become real. They become valuable because the rest of the world can experience them.

Nothing I do is perfect and it never will be. Until recently I found that frustrating and it affected me in a negative way.

When we start focusing on how awesome things are and our potential to inspire others we realize that self-doubt and insecurities have no place in our lives. I think it's ok to acknowledge them, but only if you're willing to tell them to get lost.

If you stop searching for perfection, maybe it'll find you.

After this performance at Pittsburgh First Night celebration, a gentleman approached me to say this was the best show he's ever seen in the past 6 or 7 years of coming. Remember, the world is waiting to experience what you have to offer. Don't let a stupid voice in your head get in the way.

STOP BEING AFRAID OF THINGS THAT WILL NEVER HAPPEN

Fear holds back every single one of us from doing things that we know we *should* do.

The problem is we usually fear the worst case scenario. We play a movie in our mind of all the things that could possibly go wrong and I know how easy it is to quit before you even start. The more innovative/amazing the project is, the more problems you're mind will come up saying it's not worth it.

That's fear.

In "The War of Art" Steven Pressfield calls it Resistance.

Resistance appears when we are about to do something

valuable. It wants us to stay within our comfort zone. It does anything it possibly can to keep us from taking steps toward accomplishing our goals.

It knows there are risks involved so it makes sure to remind us of everything that could go wrong.

Pressfield has an interesting take on this. He says you can be guided by your fears or 'resistance.'

He says, *"Rule of thumb: The more important a call or action is to our soul's evolution, the more Resistance we will feel toward pursuing it."*

It's the same old story of facing your fears head on.

Just remember, your biggest fears about whatever you want to do will probably never come true.

Whether you pursue that thing that you've been thinking about or not, you'll have pretty similar experiences with your fears coming true.

Your first option is to quit, give up, don't even try. Your fears won't come true because if you never try you can never fail.

On the other hand, when you go for it, the worst case scenario problems that you have been thinking about will almost never be how things play out.

Either way, your fears aren't coming true, so why are you still at option 1?

In the second option you prove to your dumb fears that you can do things despite their attempt to stop you AND you accomplish the stuff you've been longing for!

This doesn't mean the fear is defeated and goes away. You've broken through certain fears linked to that accomplishment so you've opened the gates for new goals, bigger accomplishments on your mental horizon.

Fears and resistance have been waiting for this, but you've proved them wrong before, and you'll do it again. All you have to do is tell them they're wrong and figure out a way to prove it to them. Prove it to yourself. Prove it to the world.

Fear is against you, but I'm with you. Let's do this.

What is something you've been dying to start?

Will you start today?

CAN YOU TRICK THE WORLD INTO GIVING YOU MORE LUCK?

What is luck anyway?

We see lucky people as those who get more opportunities without having to work for them. For some reason they get handed awesome things while we are struggling with no reward.

The "overnight success" got so lucky.

That friend with the awesome job got so lucky.

We have this weird desire to believe that luck actually exists. Maybe it's a good excuse for why we aren't doing awesome things. We don't need to accept any responsibility for what our life lacks. We'll just blame it on luck. Not only do we not have good luck. We've actually been on a streak of bad luck.

Now nothing is my fault. I can just blame it on luck.

OR

We can create a whole new approach to luck.

Maybe there's a finite amount of opportunities. Finite, but a MASSIVE amount.

Like rain drops. They aren't unlimited, but there's plenty to go around.

These opportunities are raining down everyday. They're desperately seeking a human to catch them and turn them into reality. If not, they have to go through the whole process again. Think of these raindrops/opportunities as your next big break seeking you out, searching for you, needing you to execute them into action. If only you could be in the right place to catch it.

So how do you capture rain drops?

You can put a small glass outside and capture some of them. A shot glass isn't going to do you much good.

That's what most of us are using.

IF WE EVEN LEAVE THE HOUSE AND GO OUT-SIDE, WE'RE ONLY CATCHING RAINDROPS IN A SHOT GLASS!

I want a bigger glass. I want a glass the size of a swimming pool with an even bigger funnel to catch even more! I want to capture every opportunity that falls out of the sky.

How big of a funnel can you create?

The raindrops might be limited, but the size of your funnel to catch them is unlimited.

Every time you meet a new person, every new skill you learn, every step you take outside of your comfort zone, every singe moment that you choose to make yourself better or just experience something new makes your funnel bigger.

You're catching more raindrops. You're getting more opportunities without working for them.

Looks like lady luck is on your side.

A lot of people are going to be jealous of you becoming an 'overnight success'. We can laugh to each other thinking about how long it really took.

In the meantime, I've got a funnel to build. I've got raindrops to catch.

And so do you, so get outside and start building.

CREATING ART IS VITAL

If you've been connected to any source of information (you're reading a book you probably ordered from the internet), you're getting bombarded with trash disguised as something that someone says you need. Advertisers and 'news' outlets are filling your brain with anything it takes to keep you clicking back for more. I'm not selling you anything, so you can trust me... Or can you? Maybe I'm just as bad as buzzfeed top 10 articles. I hope not.

But isn't it funny how we can't help ourselves from being attracted to the most terrible things? We know we shouldn't want to look, but we can't stop ourselves!

Take a glance at your Facebook feed and notice what most of the stories are. Mine is full of crime stories, police violence, and various other nonsense that I keep getting sucked into. Someone posts a controversial post and I start to get angry at these people I don't even know who are posting idiotic comments! I'm physically getting angry at strangers talking about something I don't even care about.

But we're not doomed. People are creating good art and the masses are watching. I know this is true because of shows like Ellen, puppy youtube videos and various other good spirited links that pop up.

It's vital for every one of us to create art every day. Maybe you've never picked up a paintbrush. That's cool, you don't want to see me try to paint anything. Art isn't about taking a brush or a pen to paper.

Art is creating something today that didn't exist yesterday. Maybe it's a smile on someone's face. Maybe it's a smile on your face.

For me, creating art looks like so many different things.

I'm lucky that I get paid to perform my live show all over the world. I get to share my talents with people of all ages and make them smile. Not having to go to a 'normal' job gives me freedom to create other things almost every day. I approach everything I do with my audience in mind. I want to inspire and motivate people to do cool things with their life.

I get to interview amazing performers, artists and travelers regularly on my podcast. I don't get paid to create a podcast (and a ton of time and work goes into every episode). Is it worth it? Absolutely. If one person is inspired by the people I talk to, it was worth it.

I write a blog, again, never getting paid for it. Worth it? Yup.

I make videos where I get to share experiences that other people might not get to do. It's all about broadening your perspective and increasing the size of your funnel to catch more opportunities. I want everyone to experience awesome stuff every day.

What do you have brewing inside you that the world needs to experience? Maybe you're an artist in one of the traditional senses - a painter, illustrator, musician, film maker or a photographer...

More likely, you're an artist of human experience. Your gift is being able to talk to strangers, or make your friends smile at silly things, or maybe you're really good at listening and comforting people.

Your art isn't your leisure. It's your duty. You have been blessed with talents and gifts that the world needs.

The internet isn't going away and neither are crappy posts fighting for your attention. You can accept them OR you can fight back by creating something awesome instead of consuming something terrible.

We can win, but we've go to do it together. Together we can make things better.. with art.

Someone needs you.

I need you.

Keep creating.

What is your 'art'? What are you creating today that never existed before?

NO ONE CARES HOW GOOD YOU ARE

Being really good doesn't make you stand out. It's assumed and expected that if you're offering something, it's going to be close to perfect. Now that we have access to an unlimited amount of information, our product or service needs to be really good. It's too easy for people to look up reviews or find out everything about you to offer something that isn't perfect.

Just being really good is not enough. You need to be the best at whatever you do. That's a given.

But not only the best.

You've got to be 10 times better than your competition. Otherwise, who cares?

You probably don't make phones, but let's use it as an example. Is it enough for your phone to be the best at connecting you with people?

Nope.

It's EXPECTED that your new phone will work perfectly, get great service in the middle of no where, and have great battery life. How do you stand out so people *need* what you're offering? Apple made it ACCESSIBLE to everyone. You don't need instructions. They don't even come with them!

I remember my old flip phone that had a 200 page user guide and all it did was make phone calls! The iPhone in your pocket can control your toaster to have a bagel ready for you when you arrive home (of course while using your device as a GPS to get you home while streaming ANY SONG EVER CREATED).

AND THERE'S BARELY A USER MANUAL.

You don't need to know how to do anything.

Need directions? Touch the thing that looks like a map. Done.

Apple offered all this and somehow made it COOL on top of it. In 2007-2009, having an iPhone was a conversation starter. Everyone wanted to hold it in their hands. "Look, there's no buttons!"

So don't worry about proving to anyone that you're the best.

Just be the best.

Than figure out how to be 10x better.

Or cooler.

Everyone wants to be cool.

I'm not the best juggler, in fact most professional jugglers are 10x better than I am, but I'm still getting booked. Remember that "better" doesn't always mean technically more skilled. Sometimes better means good marketing, or sometimes it really does just mean being cool. Look how cool I am.

YOU CAN'T STAY WHERE YOU ARE AND GO WHERE YOU'RE TRYING TO GO

Do cool things keep happening in your life when you're just going about your day?

Maybe they do, but if you're like most people, that's not how things work out. Every day looks the same because we get into routines that we feel comfortable with. We like the consistency of knowing what to expect. When we do the same things we did yesterday, today will turn out the same. Maybe it wasn't an incredible day but you didn't die so your biology says it was a success.

"Do that again. Keep having days that you don't die," something in our brain tells us.

So we do what we did yesterday so we don't die.

We never leave our comfort zone. When we do, sometimes it actually feels like dying.. or that we'd rather die. That sounds extreme, but it's so true.

As I'm writing this, I'm noticing how much I'm talking to myself and trying to take my own advice. Everything I've accomplished is a direct result of taking a leap of faith.

It's scary. That never goes away.

In a recent conversation, I talked about some of the things I've accomplished. There's plenty that I'm very proud of. Creating a show that tours around the world... and people pay me, hosting a podcast, writing a blog, collaborating with artists to create my clothing line betweendreamsclothing.com, and so many moments with friends and strangers I'll remember forever.

All of these things took a huge investment to turn them into reality. Sometimes an investment of straight up money, but usually just an investment of my thoughts and energy.

Take ONE thing every day that scares you. The more it scares you, the more important it is for you to do. Make the decision to take some kind of action on that thing.

Start today.

What's the worst that can happen?

You probably won't die.

If you start to live outside your comfort zone, even just for a moment each day, that comfort zone will get bigger and bigger. Each time you push, it reacts by getting bigger. Things that terrify you today might be some of your favorite activities next year.

Keep not dying.

But remember to start living.

HOW CAN YOU GET A LITTLE BETTER EVERY DAY?

Big improvements, or changes of any kind, never happen overnight. When we see someone (or ourselves) go through a big change, we're seeing the results of many tiny changes adding up.

Whether it's losing weight, gaining weight, or acquiring a new skill, everything happens in tiny steps.

At first there's some instant changes. It's what people call beginner's luck and it's there to help us not quit after the first day.

But then it gets more challenging.

When the beginner's luck wears off, life seems to throw us a test to see how bad we really want it.

The first challenge we see is the initial plateau. After we see progress at first, inevitably we'll hit a wall where things slow down (or move backwards it often seems).

I don't have an answer to why this happens or really an answer to how to avoid it. It happens. Always.

There's nothing you can do to stop it so you have to work through it. Think back to when you first started. Maybe you you've lost some enthusiasm since then. Figure out a way to get excited about your work and get through it.

The light on the other side of the tunnel is closer than you think. Your next step might be the one that takes you to the next level.

You don't know which little idea in your head might be the one to change the world, so you've got to get as many of them out into the world as possible.

There are things you can create that no one else in the world can. Don't be selfish with you gifts, talents, and skills.

Create something today and assume it'll be the thing that changes the world.

AN INSPIRATIONAL QUOTE THAT ISN'T TERRIBLE

Most inspirational quotes are really dumb, but this one I actually love.

"I always wonder why birds choose to stay in the same place when they can fly anywhere on the earth.

Then I ask myself the same question"

-Harun Yahya

I'm very guilty of often seeing things in a 'grass is always greener' perspective. I think about how awesome other people have it and how I'm always missing out on some of the best things (no matter how awesome things are going, most people are envious of others).

I know this is a common thing for a lot of people. I know my life is someone else's 'greener grass' because people often tell me straight up they wish they were doing something like what I'm doing. They see the instagram version so they don't realize my day-to-day is probably pretty similar to theirs.

Is instagram/facebook/snapchat the problem?

Are we sizing up our everyday lives to how we imagine others to be living? Sometimes I look back through my instagram and it impresses even me! It looks like I'm constantly out exploring the world and visiting exotic places. Don't get me wrong, I'm lucky that this does happen, but NOT EVERYDAY.

We look at birds and think about how free they are. They can just decide to fly away to where ever they want.

"Flying away" means different things for everyone. For some of us it's quite literal and we want to physically travel and experience the world from different viewpoints.

For others it's just experiencing new things or experiencing common things in a new way. For this we don't need to "fly" anywhere. We just need the imagination and creativity to get out of our mental ruts that we've fallen into over time.

Is there somewhere you wish you lived or could travel to? We all have these fantasies.

I want to live somewhere new everyday.

But sometimes I think to myself, and I urge you to do the same, what exactly would I be doing if I were in these particular places?

I quickly realize that I can be doing just about everything I want exactly where I currently am. It's often just an excuse to be lazy or to procrastinate when I say I need to live in a different city or need more resources or whatever else I see people on instagram with.

There's another quote that goes something like "Someone, somewhere is dreaming of the life you have now."

Don't let them down.

Live it up.

Start flying... even if that means staying right where you are.

THE GUY WHO INVENTED THE SHIP ALSO INVENTED THE SHIPWRECK

I don't know who initially said this, but I heard Seth Godin say it in a recent talk. What if you put yourself out there with an idea or a creation and it gets rejected?

What if the thing you're completely obsessed with that you know will be your greatest achievement actually fails?

Seth goes on to say, "You're either in or you're out. Either you want to play this game or you don't... Almost every best seller is a surprise best seller, because we have no idea what will work. Every company that breaks through and changes everything - all the experts said had no chance. Art doesn't work because we did something conventional and predictable. Art works because we connected."

It's irrelevant how flashy or fancy of a product you have created. No one cares. The only thing that we care about is connection. How can you connect us?

How many hours each day is your phone in your hand?

What are you doing on your phone?

Instagram, Facebook, Snapchat, Skype, Twitter, Tinder, email or text, the ONLY thing we obsess all day over is connecting with other people. Sometimes we even use the phone to make phone calls to directly connect with each other. Try it, it's fun.

It all comes together.

We have to do more than just show up every day. Putting yourself out there is risky. People might hate your ideas.

People might love your ideas.

This I know is true - people need your ideas.

What's the one thing in common to all the massively popular youtube videos/blogs/instagram accounts?

If you look at the comments there are tons of people leaving terribly negative comments. Often not even critiquing the actual content, but absolutely trash talking the person who created it.

Remember how many people absorbed the content and enjoyed and appreciated it that didn't comment something terrible.

For every bad comment I'm confident there were 100+ viewers that got precisely what they needed at that moment.

You don't need to create world-changing art or content. You need to create things that connect people to other people, new ideas, or just connect them to new ideas within themselves.

If you do that, you will change the world.

WHAT ARE YOU WILLING TO BE OBSESSED WITH?

Not just for a year or two. It might take 10 years. Or maybe it'll never work. Either way, you must make it worth it. The obsession needs to last through the bad times. The good times are easy.

It's hard to be louder than everyone else now that everyone has a voice. So what can we do to stand out from the crowd?

Wait until they're tired of making noise and all you've got to do is show up for everyone to hear you.

Everyone's got enthusiasm when they start. If you're not completely obsessed, it'll fade. This happens to 99% of people who start anything. If you can be the 1% who keeps going you will win just by being there.

Keep showing up. Some days it'll suck, but remember those are the most important days.

WHERE DO WE GO FROM HERE?

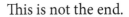

This is not the end.

This is only the beginning.

It's always only the beginning. The rest of your life starts right now.

There is no destination. All we ever have is the journey.

The horizon is calling.

Answer the call.

Just go.

I created this to gather a community. It's often too easy to
let great ideas go away without ~~doing~~ sharing them with the
world. Sometimes it's a huge help to simply chat with someone
about what you're working on.

This collaborating and sharing of ideas leads to even more
amazing things you never could have imagined.

Share this book with others. Share YOUR OWN ideas with others.

After you finish reading, sign your name and if you'd like to
hear from other readers, leave your email. Maybe someone
out there is waiting for just what you have to offer.

We are a powerful group of incredible people.
We don't just dream big. We act big.
Welcome to the JUST GO GENERATION.

- Chris

ISBN 978-0692431474

AUTHOR

Chris Ruggiero

TITLE

Just Go

DATE	BORROWER'S NAME/CONTACT
May 2015	Chris Ruggiero ruggiero.christopher@gmail.com

Made in the USA
Charleston, SC
25 November 2015